Kevin Keegan

Mike Wilson

Published in association with The Basic Skills Agency

Hodder & Stoughton

A MEMBER OF THE HODDER HEADLINE GROUP

Acknowledgements
Cover: Steve Mitchell/Empics

Photos: p iv © Neal Simpson/Empics; p3 © The Observer/Hulton Getty; pp 6, 9, 13 © Peter Robinson/Empics; p19 © David Hewitson/Empics; p22 © Matthew Ashton/Empics; p26 © Ross Kinnaird/Allsport

Every effort has been made to trace copyright holders of material reproduced in this book. Any rights not acknowledged will be acknowledged in subsequent printings if notice is given to the publisher.

Orders; please contact Bookpoint Ltd, 39 Milton Park, Abingdon, Oxon OX14 4TD. Telephone (44) 01235 400414, Fax: (44) 01235 400454. Lines are open from 9.00–6.00, Monday to Saturday, with a 24 hour message answering service. Email address: orders@bookpoint.co.uk

British Library Cataloguing in Publication Data
A catalogue record for this title is available from the British Library

ISBN 0 340 80085 2

First published 2001

| Impression number | 10 9 8 7 6 5 4 3 2 1 |
| Year | 2007 2006 2005 2004 2003 2002 2001 |

Typeset by SX Composing DTP, Rayleigh, Essex.
Printed in Great Britain for Hodder & Stoughton Educational, a division of Hodder Headline Plc, 338 Euston Road, London NW1 3BH by Redwood Books, Trowbridge, Wilts.

Contents

Kevin Keegan as England manager.

Kevin Keegan was the hero
of Liverpool's star-studded team
in the 1970s.

He helped Liverpool to win
the FA Cup and the European Cup.

He was Captain of England
and later Manager of England.
He was European Footballer of the Year
two years running.

He was the man
who saved Newcastle United – twice.
Once as a player and
once as a manager.

He got an OBE in 1982.

As a player, he did it all.

Now that Kevin Keegan has resigned
as England Manager
what will he do next?
Only time will tell.

But first . . .
his life story.

1   The Boy

Kevin Keegan
was born on 14 February, 1951.
He grew up in Doncaster,
in Yorkshire.

Kevin is his middle name.
His first name is Joseph,
after his dad, Joe.

His dad was a miner
from Newcastle.
He moved to Doncaster
looking for work down the pit.

Kevin's family were not well off.
He grew up in a house
with no electricity.
It also had no toilet or bathroom!

As a boy,
Kevin was football mad.
He wanted to be a goalkeeper,
but he was too small.

Kevin's height didn't stop him being a great goal-scorer.

He was so small,
he couldn't get a paper round.
He couldn't reach all the letter boxes!

As he grew up
he knew he wanted to be a footballer.
Everyone said he was too short,
but Kevin didn't let that stop him.

He worked out.
He trained with weights
until he was fitter and stronger
than the other boys.

He was brave and strong.
He was very fast and quick-thinking.

He didn't smoke or drink.
He liked marathon running.

He also worked for hours
on his ball control.
He jumped higher than other, taller players.
He scored lots of goals with his head.

And he never stopped running.

2   The Player

When he was 16,
Kevin signed for Scunthorpe.
Scunthorpe was in the old Fourth Division.

He got paid £4.50 a week.
Even in those days,
this was not a lot of money!
Scunthorpe was a long way
from Doncaster.
Every day Kevin had to get two buses.
Then he had to hitch a lift.

Kevin stayed at Scunthorpe
for five years.

During this time
one or two clubs had spotted him.
They could tell he was going to be a star.

Kevin signed for Scunthorpe United when he was only
sixteen. He's second on the left in the second row up.

Arsenal wanted him.
Then Millwall,
and Preston North End
(who were a big club at the time).

But it was Liverpool
who signed him in 1971.

After one or two warm-up matches,
Kevin went straight into the first team.

And the glory days began.

3 Liverpool

Kevin started at Liverpool in 1971.
The Liverpool manager
was the great Bill Shankly.
He is famous for saying:

'Football is not a matter of life and death.
It's much more important than that.'

He is also famous for building
the great Liverpool football sides of the 1970s.

Kevin looked up to Shankly.
He loved him like a father.
He learned a lot from him.

He learned all about football.
About being a manager.
How to inspire players.
How to be honest.
How to say just what you think.

Bill Shankly was one of the best football managers
of the 1970s.

Kevin scored in his first game
for Liverpool.
It was shown on *Match of the Day*.
After that,
he never looked back.

He helped Liverpool
win the League in 1973, 1976 and 1977.
They won the FA Cup in 1974,
the UEFA Cup in 1973 and 1976,
and the European Cup in 1977.

Kevin Keegan was voted
Footballer of the Year in 1975–6.

He was European Footballer of the Year
in 1978–9 and 1979–80.

By this time
Kevin had left Liverpool.
He was sold for a record
half a million pound fee.
He was playing for Hamburg SV
in Germany.

4 Hamburg and Home Again

It was a brave move to go to Germany.
It was hard work.
He had to move his wife Jean to Hamburg.
He had to prove himself.
He had to learn German.

To make it worse,
Hamburg played Liverpool
in a friendly match.
Liverpool won 6–0!

Hamburg won the German League
in 1979.
They got to the European Cup Final in 1980
but they lost 1–0
to Nottingham Forest.

By 1980 and after three years in Germany,
Kevin and Jean decided to come back home.
Kevin had not found
the big success he had wanted.

Kevin began to plan for the future
and for life after football.

For two years he played for Southampton.
Southampton was not a very big club.
(Kevin could have signed for Juventus!)

It meant Kevin and Jean could relax.
They could spend time horse-riding.

Then Kevin was injured.
It seemed his playing days
were almost over.
Yet he still scored 30 goals
in his last season with Southampton.
Not a bad way to end his career!

Then came the call from the North East.
Newcastle United were struggling
in the old Division Two.

They wanted Kevin to save them.

Kevin's great football skills helped him to become a great manager. Here he is in the 1980 England football squad (second from left) along with Glen Hoddle (fourth from left, top row).

5 Back to Newcastle

Kevin was 31 when he moved
back to Newcastle.
He was England captain.
Now he became captain
of Newcastle United as well.

Manchester United wanted to sign him,
but he went to Newcastle instead.
Back to his roots in the North East.

Kevin scored in his first three matches
for Newcastle.

The club didn't go up
to the old First Division,
but they didn't go down either.
They finished fifth.
In the next season, 1983–4,
Newcastle were promoted.

Kevin was the hero of the day.

He had done what he set out to do.
Now it was time to get out –
while he was still at the top.

Kevin retired from football
for the next eight years.
At the time he had no plans
to be a football manager.

Kevin went to live in Marbella,
in Spain.

He played tennis,
and a lot of golf.
He did some work,
talking about football on TV.

Mainly he just sat in the sun,
and relaxed with his family.

Then, in 1991,
he bought a farm
in the south of England.
He planned to breed horses.

After a while Kevin knew
that he had to get back to work.

It had taken eight years –
but he had to get back to football.

6   A Call for Help

It was January 1992
when the call came
from Newcastle United.
Once again, the club was in a bad way.

They were bottom
of the old Division Two.
It looked like they would go down.
They were losing 4–0
to teams like Oxford and Southend.

They needed Kevin to save them again.

Kevin agreed.
There were only two jobs in football
that he wanted.
Manager of England,
and manager of Newcastle United.

In the last game of the season
Newcastle scored in extra time.
It was the winning goal.
It was enough to stop them
going down.

Kevin was the hero yet again.

Keegan had the respect
of his players.
He inspired them.
They gave him 100 per cent.
(Just as Bill Shankly had inspired him
to give 100 per cent.)

As manager,
Kevin spent the team's money well.
He took Robert Lee to Tyneside,
and Andy Cole.

Newcastle won promotion in style.
They beat Leicester 7–1
and stormed into the Premier League.

7   The Premier League

In the Premiership,
Kevin went on spending money.

He bought Les Ferdinand, David Ginola,
Tino Aprilla and Alan Shearer.
(Alan Shearer cost a world record
£15 million.)

In five years,
Kevin spent £61 million.

He was the most successful manager
Newcastle had ever had.
He had a better record – home and away –
than anyone else.

Yet he never won a trophy.

In 1996, Newcastle lost a 12-point lead.
They lost the League to Manchester United.
Kevin had drive.
He had the will to win
'I'd just love it if we beat them!'
But it was not enough.

The problem was at the back.

Kevin bought Alan Shearer for £15 million!

If Newcastle scored two goals,
they let in three at the other end.

If they scored three goals,
they let in four.

The team was like the manager.
They just could not sit on a 1–0 lead.
They just could not play safe.

Kevin left Newcastle United
in January 1997.
He didn't say why.
It seemed he fell out
with the business men at the club.

Kevin had quit before.
Once it had been after a month in the job.
Once after a year.
This time, he went for good.
He said: 'It was five years in wonderland.'

He didn't have a chance
to say goodbye to the fans.
Not until he went back
for Peter Beardsley's farewell match
in January 1999.

Soon after he left Newcastle,
Kevin met Mohammed Al Fayed.

Al Fayed is a big business man.
He owns the top London shop, Harrods,
and Fulham Football Club.

Fulham was just like Newcastle had been.
It was a small club, in Division Two.
But they were aiming for the big time.

Kevin knew that Al Fayed
was just the man to make it happen.

Kevin joined Fulham as general manager
in September 1997.

Ray Wilkins, Mohammed Al Fayed and Kevin Keegan.

8   Your Country Needs You

Glenn Hoddle lost his job
as England team manager
in February 1999.
Everyone wanted Kevin to take the job –
the fans, the players, the FA.
And Kevin wanted the job.

He took over just for a few months.
Just to get England
to the European Championships in 2000.

He tried to be fair to Mohammed Al Fayed.
He tried to stay on at Fulham.
Fulham came top of Division Two.
They had a record 101 points.
But Kevin couldn't do two jobs at once.

He took on the England job full-time
in May 1999.

Al Fayed said:
'England is more important
than Fulham. Or me!'

In the run up to the European Championships
England didn't do too well.
They played 10 games
and only won three of them.
They lost two
against France and against Scotland.
All the rest were draws.

England seemed short of ideas.
They seemed short of talent and flair.
A lot of their matches ended 0–0.

At the European Championships,
it was the same.
True, England beat Germany
for the first time in 34 years.
But in too many matches
they threw away the lead.

Kevin summed up:
'We spent three matches chasing a football.
When we got it, we gave it away.'

'We just did not play well enough . . .
it was not to be.'

Maybe not this time.

9 The End of the Road

In September 2000 England drew 1–1
with the World Champions France.
Yet at the same time,
England slipped down in the world rankings.
They were named as only fourteenth
in the world.

This was bad news
for the England manager.
But there was worse to come.

In October 2000, England played Germany.
It was England's first game
in the 2002 World Cup.
It was the last game
in the old Wembley Stadium.

After 15 minutes,
England went 1–0 down.
There was some sloppy defending
at a free kick.
After that, they never looked like scoring.
Kevin knew enough was enough.

The England/Germany match was Kevin Keegan's last
match as the England manager.

It was Kevin's last game
as England manager.

'I'm just not up to the job,' he said later.
'I haven't got what it takes at this level.
I'm not the man to take it a stage further.'

This was a big shock
to the players, the FA and the fans.
Even Kevin's wife had no idea
what was on his mind.

Four days later England met Finland.
It was their next big World Cup qualifier.
Another 0–0 draw.

Many fans felt that Kevin had let the team down
by going when he did.
But Kevin had done it for the fans.

'The England fans wanted me for this job,'
he said, 'so I took it.'
'Now the fans are telling me to go . . .
It's the end of the road.'

Kevin does not like
to be on the losing side.
That's why Kevin quit the England job
the way he did.
He is a proud man.
He didn't want to carry on
failing his country.

'I will look for a life
away from football,' he said.
Yet there has been talk
of a business deal.
Kevin would open football theme parks
all over the UK.

Whatever he does,
you can be sure Kevin Keegan
will give 100 per cent.

And he will always be
in the winning team.